AF270654

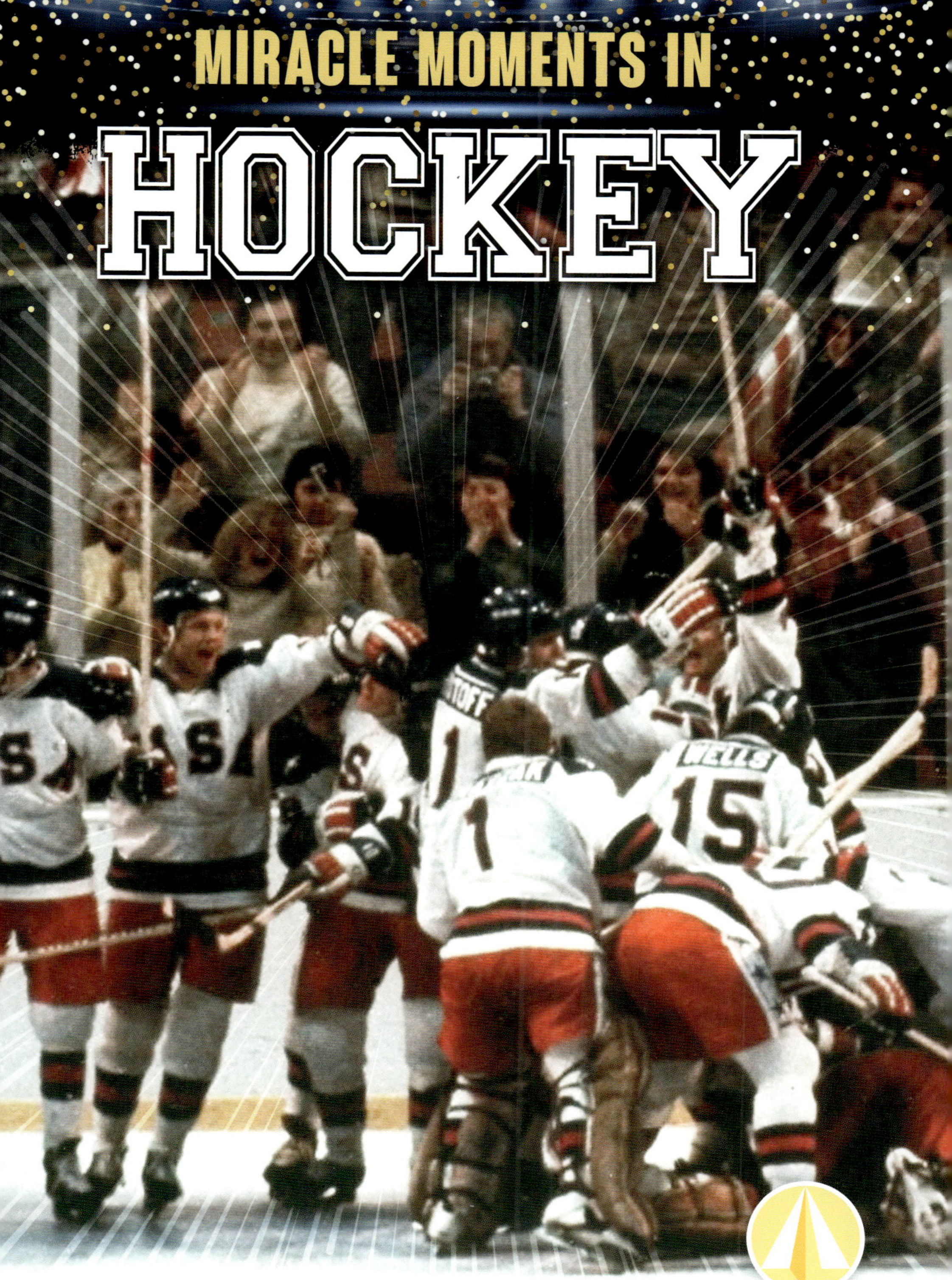

MIRACLE MOMENTS IN
HOCKEY
KENNY ABDO
Fly!
An Imprint of Abdo Zoom
abdobooks.com

abdobooks.com

Published by Abdo Zoom, a division of ABDO, P.O. Box 398166, Minneapolis, Minnesota 55439. Copyright © 2022 by Abdo Consulting Group, Inc. International copyrights reserved in all countries. No part of this book may be reproduced in any form without written permission from the publisher. Fly!™ is a trademark and logo of Abdo Zoom.

Printed in the United States of America, North Mankato, Minnesota.
052021
092021

Photo Credits: AP Images, Everett Collection, Granger Collection, Icon Sportswire, iStock, Newscom, Shutterstock
Production Contributors: Kenny Abdo, Jennie Forsberg, Grace Hansen
Design Contributors: Dorothy Toth, Neil Klinepier

Library of Congress Control Number: 2020919712

Publisher's Cataloging-in-Publication Data

Names: Abdo, Kenny, author.
Title: Miracle moments in hockey / by Kenny Abdo
Description: Minneapolis, Minnesota : Abdo Zoom, 2022 | Series: Miracles in sports | Includes online resources and index.
Identifiers: ISBN 9781098223212 (lib. bdg.) | ISBN 9781098223915 (ebook) | ISBN 9781098224264 (Read-to-Me ebook)
Subjects: LCSH: Hockey--History--Juvenile literature. | Hockey--Records--Juvenile literature. | Sports--History--Juvenile literature. | Miracles--Juvenile literature. | Curiosities and wonders--Juvenile literature.
Classification: DDC 796.963--dc23

TABLE OF CONENTS

HOCKEY

From North America to the Czech Republic, hockey makes an ice-cold sport red hot with excitement.

Curved stick and ball games can be traced back 4,000 years to Egypt. Canada takes ownership of putting it on ice late in the 19th **century**.

In that time, miracles ranging from **barn burners** to broken-legged shots have etched themselves into hockey history.

DO YOU BELIEVE?

In 1964, Maple Leafs Bob Baun left the ice in Game 6 of the **Stanley Cup**. He had broken a leg. Baun returned to the game in **overtime playoffs**. He scored the game-winning goal. The team went on to win the Stanley Cup.

During the 1980 Winter Olympics, the less-experienced Team USA beat the indestructible **Soviets**. It is known as the "Miracle on Ice."

The final score was 4-3, leading to announcer Al Michael's iconic final call, "Do you believe in miracles?!"

The Capitals and Islanders performed their own Easter Sunday miracle in 1987. The game started at 7:30 PM on Saturday night and ended at 1:58 AM. It is the longest Game 7 in **Stanley Cup playoff** history. The Islanders won the Easter Epic.

Washington
Capitals
22

Blackhawks Patrick Kane broke a 49-year curse in 2010. He scored the winning goal against the Flyers in **overtime**. Nobody saw the shot go in because of the angle. "Phantom goal" or not, the Blackhawks won the **Stanley Cup**!

KIE'S & PETE'S
BLA
PETE'S
ckpot.
$
BALL
ERPLAY
MI
nty
Reebok
17

PyeongChang 2018
USA
CCM

During the 2018 Winter Olympics, the USA Women's team did the unthinkable. They went up against Canada, who nabbed victories in the last four matchups. USA's Jocelyne Lamoureux-Davidson scored the winning shot in the sixth round of intense **shootouts**.

LEGACY

The "Miracle on Ice" made more than sports history. It has been recreated in made for TV movies to documentaries. In 2004, the hit movie *Miracle* was released on the big screen and starred Kurt Russell.

Fans of hockey watch for players to do the impossible on the ice, making it **breakaway** entertainment for all.

GLOSSARY

barn burner – a sporting event that is very intense and exciting.

breakaway – when a player has the puck and an open skating lane to the goal with no one in front of them.

overtime – additional minutes added to a tied-up game giving each team a chance to win.

shootout – in hockey, a tie-breaker method where 3 players from each team attempt a shot on the opponent's goalie. If the score remains tied, the shootout moves into a sudden death round.

Stanley Cup playoff – an elimination tournament played each year by qualifying teams in the NHL. The winner takes home the Stanley Cup trophy.

Soviets – the Soviet national ice hockey team that won nearly every world championship and Olympic tournament between 1954 and 1991.

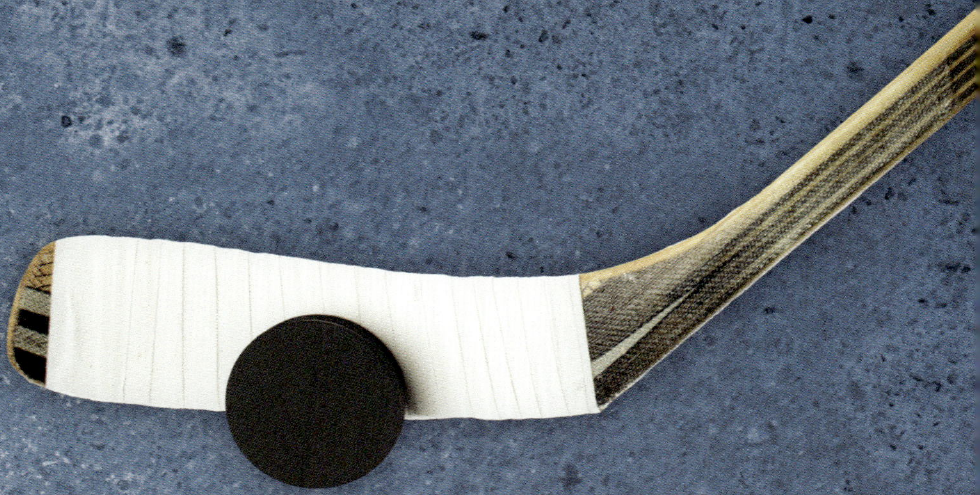

ONLINE RESOURCES

To learn more about miracle moments in hockey, please visit **abdobooklinks.com** or scan this QR code. These links are routinely monitored and updated to provide the most current information available.

INDEX